# Why Can't I Jump Very High?

**A Book About Gravity**

Written by Kamal S. Prasad
Illustrated by Aurore Simonnet

Science Square
Publishing

Santa Rosa

All rights reserved.

Copyright © 2004 by Kamal S. Prasad.

Illustrations copyright © 2004 by Aurore Simonnet.

Published by Science Square Publishing.
*http://www.sciencesquare.com*

No part of this book may be reproduced, copied or transmitted in any form or by any means, mechanical or electronic, without prior permission from Science Square Publishing. For information regarding permissions, please write to Science Square Publishing, 4683 Quigg Dr., #322, Santa Rosa, CA 95409, USA.

While the concepts presented in this book are non-fiction, the characters and events depicted herein are fictitious and any similarities to any persons or events are purely coincidental.

Library of Congress Control Number: 2004090021

ISBN: 0-9740861-5-0

Printed in Hong Kong

First printing in 2004.
08 07 06 05 04    5 4 3 2 1

Printed on recycled paper using soy-based inks.

*For all the children in the world and the scientists of tomorrow.*

*For our parents, teachers, family and friends who encouraged us to pursue our dreams.*

Ms. Spencer was walking through the playground during recess, observing the different activities of students. When she got to the basketball court, she paused to watch a group of students trying to slam-dunk a basketball. The students were not having a lot of luck. Some of the students playing were from her class. Ramon, one of her students, noticed Ms. Spencer watching them play. He had just made an unsuccessful attempt to slam-dunk the basketball.

"Ms. Spencer, why can't I jump very high?" Ramon asked. "I'm a good athlete and I'm tall but I cannot ever jump high enough to slam-dunk the basketball."

"Well Ramon, it is gravity that holds us on the ground and keeps us from jumping too high," answered Ms. Spencer.

"What is gravity?" inquired Suzie who was waiting for her turn to try to slam-dunk the basketball. "I've heard the word before but never understood it."

"Gravity is a **force** that brings two objects, or things, together," replied Ms. Spencer. "Just like when you pull a cart towards you, gravity is pulling you towards the ground except that there are no ropes attached. The larger the object's mass, the greater its gravitational pull. Earth is a massive object. That is why everything sticks to the ground so well."

"Bummer," sighed Ramon. "I wish there were no gravity."

"Well, Ramon," said Ms. Spencer. "If gravity stopped pulling on us, then we would not be able to do everyday things like walking and riding bicycles, or even playing basketball."

"What if Earth had less gravity?" asked Suzie. "Like the moon! I saw **astronauts** on the moon jumping really high on a TV program once!"

"That is a good point, Suzie," continued Ms. Spencer. "The moon has less mass than Earth, which makes the moon's gravity about six times less than Earth's. This means that you could jump six times higher on the moon than you do here on Earth. But you must have also noticed that the astronauts were wearing special suits while they were out on the moon. That is because the moon has very little **atmosphere**. The moon's smaller gravity cannot keep air from flowing out into space. In fact, gravity here on Earth also helps keep the air that we breathe from escaping into space. So, we should be thankful for gravity."

Suddenly the school bell rang and recess was over.

Back in the classroom, after the students had settled down, Ms. Spencer addressed the class, "During recess some students and I started talking about gravity, what it is and what it does." She repeated the discussion that she had with Ramon and Suzie at the basketball court.

"Now, Class, tell me, what are your thoughts about gravity? Do you have any questions?" Ms. Spencer asked the students. "Yes, Alan?"

"How does Earth know whether it's pulling on a rock or a piece of paper?" asked Alan. "Gravity is what makes a rock fall faster than a piece of paper, doesn't it?"

"That is an important question to ask, Alan," said Ms. Spencer. "People, for a long time, thought that everything wanted to be as close to Earth as possible, but heavier things wanted to be closer to Earth more than lighter ones. That is the reason they thought things like rocks fell to Earth faster than things like pieces of paper."

"The ancient Greek philosopher **Aristotle** is the person who came up with this idea," she continued. "This way of looking at gravity was changed when a scientist named **Isaac Newton** showed that the force of gravity created by an object affects other objects in exactly the same way. This means that a pebble and a piece of paper dropped from the same height will hit the ground at the same time."

Ms. Spencer paused to let the students ponder this information. At that moment, Alan jumped out of his chair holding a piece of paper and a marble that he dug out of his pocket.

"But look!" Alan insisted as he dropped the piece of paper and the marble from about the same height and at the same time. The marble headed straight down to the ground while the paper floated from side to side before settling on the ground several seconds later. "The marble hit the ground way before the paper!"

"What a wonderful demonstration!" remarked Ms. Spencer. "Presentations like these caused people to believe Aristotle. Now let me repeat the demonstration but instead of a flat piece of paper, let's make it into a ball."

Ms. Spencer walked over to where Alan had dropped the marble and the paper, picked them up, and crumpled the piece of paper into a ball.

"We have to make sure that air will not affect our **experiment**," said Ms. Spencer. "We do not want any unwanted **variables** to change our results. As it is a pretty calm day, we do not have to worry about the wind interrupting our experiment."

As Ms. Spencer got ready to drop the two objects, the class calmed down and watched, anxious to see what would happen. She then dropped the marble and the ball of paper from about the same height.

"The ball of paper hit the floor first!" shouted out one student.

"No, I think they fell at the same time!" exclaimed another.

"Let's try it again," suggested Ms. Spencer. She picked up the two objects and repeated the experiment. Again, there were many different answers but more students now seem to be agreeing that the two objects hit the floor at the same time.

"Why do you think the ball of paper fell faster than the flat piece of paper?" Ms. Spencer asked the class.

"It seems to me that the flat piece of paper catches more air than the paper ball," volunteered Ruth.

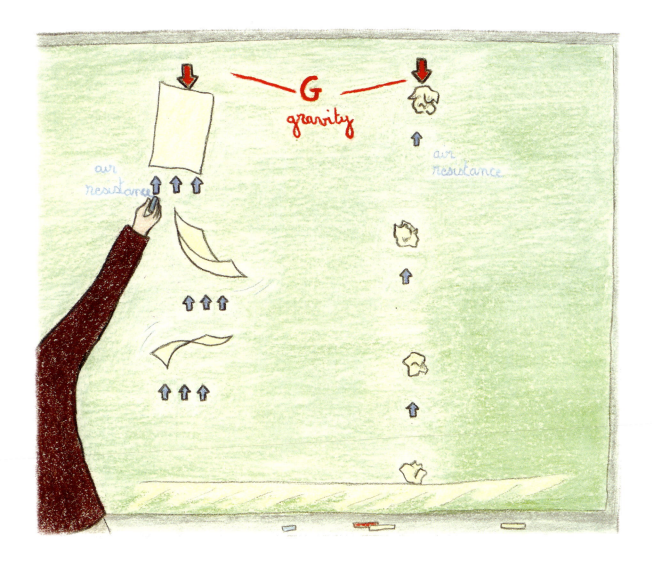

"That is exactly correct, Ruth," said Ms. Spencer with a smile. "Air, even though we cannot see it, causes falling things to slow down. This force working against gravity is called air **friction**. The more area on an object air can catch onto, the more time it takes the object to fall to the ground."

"Why don't you all try this experiment for yourselves," said Ms. Spencer. "Use different objects, and make sure to drop them from the same height and at the same time. Be careful not to hurt yourself or anyone else."

After Ms. Spencer had allowed some time for the students to repeat the experiment by themselves, she asked the class to return to their seats.

"Does anyone have any other questions?" she inquired once the class had settled down.

"How far does the force of gravity go? I mean, the astronauts in space don't feel gravity, right?" asked Tina.

"Actually, Tina, as far as we know, the gravitational force created by an object goes on forever," replied Ms. Spencer. "It is gravity that keeps the astronauts from floating out into space, and it is gravity that keeps the moon in **orbit** around Earth."

"If Earth's gravity is pulling on the moon, why doesn't the moon fall to Earth?" inquired Tina.

"The force of gravity created by something becomes smaller the farther away you move from it," answered Ms. Spencer. "The moon and astronauts in space are far from Earth, so the force of gravity they feel is a lot less than what we feel here on the surface of our planet."

After a brief pause, Ms. Spencer spoke again, "Now, Class, let me ask you a question. How do you think we know that it is Earth's gravity that holds the moon in orbit around Earth?"

There were puzzled looks on almost all the children's faces.  Some seemed like they might have an answer, but they were not very certain.

"There is a demonstration, which I can do to help answer that question," Ms. Spencer said as she pulled out some string and a chalkboard eraser from the desk drawer.  She tied the eraser to one end of the string.  Standing in front of the classroom, she started swinging the eraser in a circle.  After a few seconds she stopped.

"Okay, Class, what would have happened if I had let go of the string while I was swinging the eraser?" she asked.

"The eraser would have flown off," answered the class almost in unison.

"And what kept the eraser from flying off?" asked Ms. Spencer.

"The string," replied the class.

"That is correct. The string that was attached to my hand," said Ms. Spencer. "You can think of my hand as Earth, the string as the force of gravity created by my hand and the eraser as the moon. The moon would go flying off but the gravity created by Earth makes it go around Earth instead. Does this help you understand that gravity keeps the moon in orbit?"

Most of the class nodded their heads while some did not seem too sure.

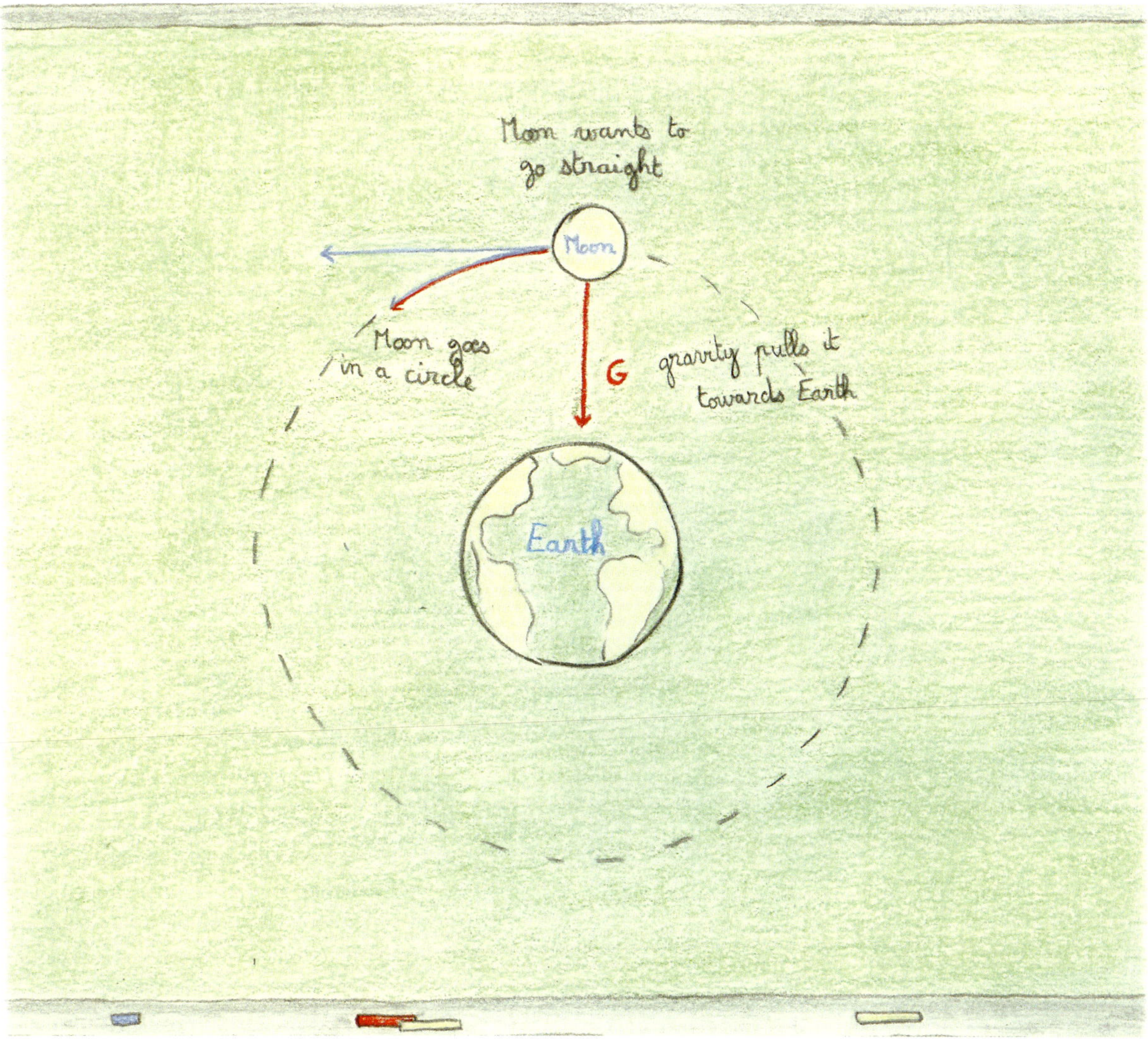

Moon wants to go straight

Moon

Moon goes in a circle

G gravity pulls it towards Earth

Earth

"You all should take some time to think about our discussion," said Ms. Spencer. "It will help you clear up questions you may have about gravity. And as always, you can ask me more questions later."

Just then, the school bell rang, reminding the class their reading hour was beginning, and that ended their discussion of gravity for that day.

# Glossary

**Aristotle** - Ancient Greek philosopher who was interested in how things worked. He tried to explain how things worked without actually doing any **experiments**. This made him get some things wrong, for example, how gravity works.

**Astronauts** - Astronauts are people who travel to outer space. They are also known as cosmonauts (Russian terminology) or taikonauts (Chinese terminology).

**Atmosphere** - is the layer of gases that usually surrounds a planet. For Earth, we call this mixture of gases air.

**Experiment** - A series of steps designed to test a **hypothesis**. This usually includes makings observations and/or taking measurements of the interaction of objects. For example, you might time how long it takes for different objects to fall to the ground from a certain height to see if it takes as long as you thought it would.

**Force** - A force is a pull or a push. For example, when you ride a bicycle, you have to push on the pedals to make the wheels turn. You are using force to make the bicycle move. Similarly, when you pull a cart you are using force.

**Friction** - A type of force that opposes movement.  For example, if you try to push a table to the left side of a room, the force of friction would be between the table's legs and the floor towards the right side of the room.

**Gravity** - is the **force** created by a **mass** that attracts other objects to that mass.  It also depends on the distance between the mass and the object.  For example, Earth's gravity attracts us to it therefore keeping us firmly on the ground, but the further we move away from Earth, the weaker its gravitional pull becomes.

**Hypothesis** - An educated guess or prediction about what might happen under certain circumstances.  For example, if you were to drop a feather and a hammer from the same height at the same time, your hypothesis might be that the hammer will hit the ground first, or it could be that they both fall together.

**Isaac Newton** - is one of the most famous physicist and mathematician that ever lived.  He came up with Newton's Three Laws of Motion and discovered the law of gravity.  He also invented a useful advanced way of doing mathematics, called calculus.

**Mass** - The amount of stuff something is made of.  The more stuff something is made of, the more mass it has.  Suppose everything in the world were made up of marbles.  In this case you would be made out of more marbles than a piece of paper because you have more mass than a piece of paper.

**Massive** - Something with a lot of mass.

**Orbit** - An elliptical path that satellites and planets take around a more **massive** object. For example, the planets in our solar system are in orbit around the sun, and the moon is a satellite in orbit around Earth.

**Variables** - are things that change in an **experiment**. For example, when you plant sunflower seeds in different types of dirt to see which dirt is best for growing sunflowers, the variable is the different types of dirt you used.

# Resources

At the Science Square Publishing website, you will find additional resources regarding gravity. There are animations, activities, and links to websites that have more information on the subject. You can even have your own questions about gravity answered by the author.

For teachers and parents, there are lesson plans, worksheets, and suggestions on ways to further engage children in critically thinking about what they are reading.

All these resources can be found at *http://www.sciencesquare.com*